Erika's Story

Erika's Story

Written by Ruth Vander Zee

Illustrated by Roberto Innocenti

A Tom Maschler Book
Jonathan Cape
London

To my children. Your stars brighten my life.

R. V. Z.

ERIKA'S STORY
A JONATHAN CAPE BOOK 0 224 07015 0

First published in 2003 by Creative Editions, an imprint of The Creative Company, 123 South Broad Street, Mankato, MN 56001 USA

First published in Great Britain by Jonathan Cape, an imprint of Random House Children's Books

This edition published 2004

10 9 8 7 6 5 4 3 2 1

RANDOM HOUSE CHILDREN'S BOOKS
61–63 Uxbridge Rd, London W5 5SA
A division of The Random House Group Ltd

RANDOM HOUSE AUSTRALIA (PTY) LTD
20 Alfred Street, Milsons Point, Sydney,
New South Wales 2061, Australia

RANDOM HOUSE NEW ZEALAND LTD
18 Poland Road, Glenfield, Auckland 10, New Zealand

RANDOM HOUSE (PTY) LTD
Endulini, 5A Jubilee Road, Parktown 2193, South Africa

THE RANDOM HOUSE GROUP Limited Reg. No. 954009
www.kidsatrandomhouse.co.uk

A CIP catalogue record for this book is available from the British Library.

Printed in Italy

Author's Note

✡

In 1995, the fiftieth anniversary of the end of World War II, I met the woman in this story. My husband and I were sitting on a kerb in Rothenburg, Germany, watching a clean-up crew gather shards of broken roof tile from the city hall. A small tornado had ripped through this lovely medieval village the night before and scattered rubble everywhere. An elderly merchant standing nearby was telling us that the storm left as much devastation as the last Allied attack of the war.

When the merchant went back to tending his shop, the lady sitting next to us introduced herself as Erika. She asked if we had been travelling. When I told her we had been

✡

studying in Jerusalem for two weeks, she said, with longing in her voice, that she had always wanted to visit Jerusalem but had never been able to afford the trip.

I noticed she was wearing a Star of David on a gold chain around her neck, so I mentioned that after our stay in Israel, we had driven through Austria and visited the concentration camp in Mauthausen. Erika told me that she had once got as far as the entrance to Dachau but could not bear to enter.

She then told me her story...

From 1933 to 1945, six million of my people were killed. Many were shot. Many were starved.

Many were burned in ovens or gassed in chambers. I was not.

✡

I was born sometime in 1944.

I do not know my birthdate.

I do not know my birth name.

I do not know in what city or country I was born.

I do not know if I had brothers or sisters.

What I do know is that when I was just a few months old, I was saved from the Holocaust.

✡

I often imagine what my family's life was like the last few weeks we spent together. I imagine my mother and father robbed of everything they owned, forced from their home, and relocated to a ghetto.

Later, perhaps we were ordered from the ghetto. My parents must have been eager to leave the barbed-wire fenced section of the city to which they had been assigned – to escape the typhus, overcrowding, filth, and starvation. But did they have any notion of where they would go next? Were they told that they were being resettled in a better place? A place where there would be food and work? Had they heard whispered rumours of death camps?

✡

28
27
27
DR
0134
Kg.

VERBOTEN

I wonder how they felt when they were herded to the railway station with hundreds of other Jews. Crammed into a cattle car. Standing room only. Did they panic when they heard the doors barred shut?

✡

The train must have travelled from one village to another through pastoral landscapes

strangely untouched by terror. How many days were we on that train? How many hours did my parents stand crushed together?

✡

I imagine my mother holding me close to protect me from the stench, the cries, the fear inside that packed car. By now she undoubtedly knew she was not heading to a place of safety.

I wonder where she stood. Was she in the middle of the car? Was my father next to her? Did he tell her to be brave? Did they talk about what to do?

✡

When did they make their decision?

Did my mother say, "Excuse me. Excuse me. Excuse me"? Did she work her way through all the people to the wooden wall of the car?

While she wrapped me tightly in a warm blanket, did she whisper my name? Did she cover my face with kisses and tell me that she loved me? Did she cry? Did she pray?

✡

As the train slowed through a village, my mother must have looked up through the opening near the top of the cattle car. With my father, she must have tried spreading the barbed wire that covered the hole. My mother must have lifted me over her head and towards the dim daylight. What happened next is the only thing I know for sure.

✡

My mother threw me from the train.

✡

25
BD
12
25

She threw me from the train onto a little patch of grass just past a railway crossing. People standing there, waiting for the train to pass, saw me hurled from that cattle car. On her way to death, my mother threw me to life.

✡

Someone standing nearby picked me up and took me to a woman who cared for me. She risked her life for me. She estimated my age and gave me a birthdate. She said my name would be Erika. She gave me a home. She fed me, clothed me, and sent me to school. She was good to me.

✡

27
26
DR
28
27

When I was twenty-one, I married a wonderful man. He lifted the sadness that often filled me, and he understood my desire to belong to a family. We had three children together, and now they have children of their own. In their faces, I see mine.

✡

It was once said that my people would be as many as the stars in the heavens. Six million of those stars fell between 1933 and 1945. Every star was one of my people whose life was savaged and whose family tree was torn apart.

✡

Today, my tree once again has roots.

✡

My star still shines.

★